DANIIL KARABUT

The Secret Lives of Ordinary People

Insights and Strategies for Personal Growth and Self-Discovery

The real voyage of discovery consists
not in seeking new landscapes, but in
having new eyes.

Marcel Proust

Contents

Foreword

As human beings, we all have inner lives often hidden from the outside world. We carry a complex web of emotions, thoughts, and experiences that shape who we are and how we interact with others. Yet, these inner lives are often not fully understood or acknowledged, even by ourselves.

"The Secret Lives of Ordinary People" seeks to explore this inner world, shed light on the complexities of human experience, and offer practical guidance for cultivating resilience, self-compassion, and well-being. In this book, you will find a wealth of insights and strategies for navigating the challenges and joys of life based on the latest research in psychology, mindfulness, and personal growth.

The topics covered in this book are broad and diverse, ranging from coping with family dynamics to practicing cognitive-behavioral therapy. However, they all share a common thread - cultivating self-awareness, empathy, and compassion for ourselves and others. By developing these qualities, we can learn to navigate the complexities of human experience with greater ease and grace.

As the author of this book, I am passionate about empowering individuals to live their best lives and discover the richness and complexity of their inner worlds. I hope this book will inspire and guide you on your growth journey, and you will come away with a greater sense of self-awareness, self-compassion, and resilience.

Thank you for joining me on this journey of personal growth and self-discovery.

Preface

As a therapist and researcher, I have spent many years exploring the complexities of human experience and the factors that contribute to well-being. Through my work, I have come to appreciate the vastness and richness of the human psyche and the importance of cultivating self-awareness, empathy, and compassion for ourselves and others.

"The Secret Lives of Ordinary People" is the culmination of this work - a guide to personal growth and self-discovery that draws on the latest research in psychology, mindfulness, and personal development. The book explores various topics relevant to individuals seeking to improve their mental, emotional, and relational well-being, from managing emotions and building healthy relationships to cultivating self-compassion and resilience.

Through this exploration, I hope to offer readers a deeper understanding of themselves and their experiences and to provide practical guidance and inspiration for cultivating inner strength and resilience. I also hope to emphasize the importance of seeking help and support when needed and to provide resources for readers to explore further.

It's important to note that this book is not intended to be a substitute for therapy or professional guidance. Instead, it's meant to be a starting point for individuals on their growth journey, a source of inspiration and advice as they navigate the complexities of human experience.

I'm honored to share this book with you, and I hope it will offer valuable insights and strategies for cultivating a more fulfilling and meaningful life. Thank you for joining me on this journey of personal growth and self-discovery.

Acknowledgement

I want to express my gratitude to the many individuals who have supported and inspired me throughout the writing of this book.

First and foremost, I would like to thank my family and friends for their unwavering support and encouragement. Your love and support have been the foundation of my personal and professional growth.

I would also like to thank my colleagues and mentors in psychology, whose insights and guidance have shaped my understanding of the human experience and informed my approach to therapy and personal growth.

I'm grateful to the many clients who have shared their experiences with me over the years and taught me so much about the resilience and strength of the human spirit.

This book is the result of a collective effort, and I'm honored to have had the opportunity to collaborate with so many talented and dedicated individuals. Thank you all for your support and encouragement and for sharing in this journey of personal growth and self-discovery.

Introduction

We all have secrets. Things we keep hidden from the world, tucked away in our minds, or buried deep within our hearts. Some of these secrets are small, like our crush on our high school teacher or the time we stole a candy bar from the corner store. Others are more significant, like the trauma we experienced as a child or the fear that we'll never be good enough.

These secrets are what make us human. They are what makes us complex, engaging, and unique. But they are also what makes us vulnerable. We fear we will be judged, rejected, or ridiculed if we reveal these secrets. So we keep them hidden, even from those closest to us.

In "The Secret Lives of Ordinary People," we explore the hidden aspects of human nature that we don't often see from the outside. Through real-life stories and examples, we delve into ordinary people's secrets, struggles, talents, and lifestyles. We explore the different kinds of secrets that people keep, the inner struggles they face, and the hidden talents they possess. We also examine the double lives they lead, their unconventional lifestyles, and the private rituals and emotions that they experience.

Through this exploration, we hope to shed light on human nature's complexity and show that we are all more alike than different. We all have secrets, struggles, and aspirations. We all have hidden talents and emotions. And we all can live rich, meaningful lives, even in adversity.

So come with us on this journey into the secret lives of ordinary people. We hope you'll come away with a deeper understanding of yourself, others, and the world around us.

Secrets People Keep: Why We Keep Them

People often have secrets they don't share with anyone, whether it's a fear, a trauma, a desire, or anything else they don't want to reveal. These secrets can be deeply personal and may impact our lives. In this chapter, we'll explore the different kinds of secrets people keep and why we keep them.

One common type of secret people keep is related to their mental health. Many people struggle with anxiety, depression, or other mental health issues, but they may hold this hidden from others for fear of being judged or stigmatized. Similarly, people may keep secrets related to their past experiences, such as abuse or neglect, for fear of being judged or ostracized.

Another common reason why people keep secrets is related to shame or embarrassment. People may feel ashamed of their desires or preferences, such as sexual fantasies, fetishes, or kinks. They may also be embarrassed about their appearance or personality traits that they feel are unattractive or undesirable.

Fear is another significant factor that contributes to people keeping secrets. People may fear judgment or criticism from others or the consequences of revealing their secrets. For example, a person who has an affair may fear losing their partner, while someone with a secret addiction may fear losing their job or social status.

People may also keep secrets to protect others. For example, a person may hold a mystery related to a friend or family member's mental health or substance abuse issue to avoid causing harm or embarrassment.

Ultimately, the reasons why people keep secrets are complex and multifaceted. While some secrets may be harmless, others can significantly affect people's mental health and well-being. In this book, we'll explore the different kinds of secrets people keep and the impact that these secrets can have on our lives. We'll also offer strategies for coping with secrets and seeking help when needed.

Inner Struggles: Coping with Anxiety, Depression, and Addiction

We all have inner struggles that we deal with daily. These struggles can range from anxiety and depression to addiction and self-doubt. While we may not always show these struggles to the outside world, they can profoundly impact our lives.

One common inner struggle that people face is anxiety. Anxiety can take many forms, from social anxiety to generalized anxiety disorder. People with anxiety may feel constant worry, fear, or unease, making it difficult to function in everyday life. They may avoid social situations, have trouble sleeping, or experience physical symptoms like headaches or stomachaches.

Another common inner struggle is depression. Depression is a severe mental health condition that can make it difficult to enjoy life and engage in activities that used to bring pleasure. People with depression may feel sad, hopeless, or empty and struggle with low energy, poor concentration, or changes in appetite or sleep patterns.

People also struggle with addiction, whether it's to drugs, alcohol, or other substances. Addiction can be a complex cycle to break, as people may use their senses to cope with underlying emotional pain or trauma. Addiction can seriously affect a person's physical and mental health, relationships, and overall well-being.

Coping with inner struggles can be challenging, but it's important to remember that help is available. Seeking professional help, such as therapy or medication, can be crucial in managing these struggles and improving one's quality of life. Other coping mechanisms may include exercise, mindfulness practices, and self-care activities.

In this chapter, we'll explore the different kinds of inner struggles that people face, including anxiety, depression, and addiction. We'll offer strategies for coping with these struggles and seeking help when needed. Sharing our efforts with others and seeking support can break down mental health stigma and create a more compassionate and understanding society.

Coping with Anxiety:

- Practice relaxation techniques like deep breathing, meditation, or progressive muscle relaxation
- Engage in physical activity, such as exercise or yoga
- Challenge negative thoughts and replace them with positive affirmations
- Talk to someone about your worries, whether it's a trusted friend or mental health professional
- Consider therapy, medication, or other forms of professional help if your anxiety is impacting your daily life

Coping with Depression:

- Engage in activities that bring you pleasure or a sense of accomplishment, even if you don't feel like it
- Seek social support from friends, family, or a support group

- Practice self-care activities like taking a warm bath or listening to music
- Challenge negative thoughts and replace them with positive affirmations
- Consider therapy, medication, or other forms of professional help if your depression is impacting your daily life

Coping with Addiction:

- Seek professional help, such as therapy or a support group
- Identify triggers and develop coping strategies to avoid or manage them
- Create a support system of friends or family who can provide accountability and encouragement
- Practice self-care activities like exercise or meditation
- Consider medication-assisted treatment if appropriate

It's important to remember that seeking help is a sign of strength, not weakness. Many resources are available for those struggling with inner struggles, including therapy, support groups, and hotlines. By seeking help and engaging in coping strategies, we can better manage these struggles and improve our overall well-being.

Family Secrets: Coping with Dysfunctional Family Dynamics

Families can be a source of love and support but also the source of family secrets and dysfunction. Family secrets can take many forms, from a history of addiction or abuse to a hidden family member or illegitimate child. These secrets can have a profound impact on individuals and the family as a whole.

One common reason why people keep family secrets is related to shame and stigma. People may fear judgment or rejection from others if they reveal their family's history or dynamics. They may also feel a sense of loyalty or obligation to keep the family secret hidden.

Family secrets can also impact family dynamics and relationships. Secrets can create a sense of distance or distrust between family members, or they may lead to resentment or anger if the secret is eventually revealed. Secrets can also contribute to dysfunctional family dynamics, such as enabling or codependent behaviors.

Coping with family secrets can be challenging, but it's important to remember that you are not alone. Seeking professional help, such as therapy or family counseling, can be crucial in managing family secrets and improving relationships. Other coping mechanisms may include setting boundaries with family members, practicing self-care, and seeking support from friends or support groups.

In this chapter, we'll explore the impact of family secrets on individuals and families and offer strategies for coping with dysfunctional family dynamics. We'll also discuss the importance of seeking professional help and the benefits of support groups. By sharing our experiences and seeking help when needed, we can break down the stigma surrounding family secrets and create healthier family dynamics.

Family secrets can have a significant impact on individuals and families. They can create a sense of shame, guilt, or fear and may impact self-esteem or mental health. Family secrets can also affect relationships, leading to distrust, resentment, or anger. In some cases, family secrets can even lead to physical or emotional abuse.

Family secrets can also impact future generations, as patterns of secrecy or dysfunctional family dynamics may be passed down. Children who grow up in families with secrets may struggle with trust or intimacy in relationships and may have difficulty forming healthy relationships with others.

Strategies for Coping with Dysfunctional Family Dynamics:

If you are struggling with family secrets or dysfunctional family dynamics, there are steps you can take to cope and improve your situation:

- Seek professional help: A therapist or family counselor can help you work through family issues and develop healthy coping strategies. They can also offer support and guidance as you navigate challenging family dynamics.
- Set boundaries: If a family member is causing harm or stress in your life, it may be necessary to set boundaries or limit

contact with them. This can help protect your well-being and prevent further damage.

- Practice self-care: Engage in activities that bring you joy and promote your mental health, such as exercise, meditation, or spending time with friends.
- Seek support: Talk to friends, support groups, or other trusted individuals who can offer empathy and understanding. Connecting with others who have had similar experiences can help you feel less alone and more supported.
- Consider family therapy: Family therapy may be helpful if multiple family members are struggling with secrets or dysfunctional dynamics. This can provide a safe space for all family members to share their experiences and work towards improved communication and understanding.

Importance of Seeking Professional Help and Benefits of Support Groups:

While coping with family secrets and dysfunctional family dynamics can be challenging, seeking professional help can offer significant benefits. Therapy or family counseling can provide a safe, non-judgmental space to work through family issues and develop healthy coping strategies. Support groups can also provide empathy and understanding and offer community to those struggling with family secrets.

Fear of Judgment and Shame: Overcoming the Stigma of Mental Health

One of the biggest obstacles that prevent people from seeking help for their mental health issues is the fear of judgment and shame. Despite growing awareness and understanding of mental health issues, there is still a significant stigma surrounding mental illness, making it difficult for people to reach out for help.

People with mental health issues may fear being labeled or judged by others and feel ashamed or embarrassed about their struggles. This can lead to a reluctance to seek help, worsening mental health symptoms, and leading to long-term negative consequences.

It's important to remember that mental health issues are common and treatable conditions, just like physical illnesses. Seeking help for mental health concerns is a sign of strength, not weakness. Many resources are available for those struggling with mental health issues, including therapy, medication, and support groups.

Breaking down the stigma surrounding mental illness requires a collective effort. We can all play a role in reducing the stigma by educating ourselves and others about mental health issues, speaking out against discrimination and stigma, and offering empathy and support to those struggling.

In this chapter, we'll explore the impact of stigma and shame on mental health and offer strategies for overcoming the fear of judgment and shame. We'll also discuss the importance of seeking help for mental health concerns and the benefits of mental health treatment.

Impact of Stigma and Shame on Mental Health:

The stigma surrounding mental illness can have a significant impact on mental health. People who experience stigma and shame may be less likely to seek help, which can lead to worsened mental health symptoms and increased distress. Stigma can also lead to discrimination and exclusion, making it more difficult for people with mental health issues to participate fully in society.

Strategies for Overcoming the Fear of Judgment and Shame:

If you are struggling with the fear of judgment and shame related to mental health, there are steps you can take to cope and overcome these feelings:

- Educate yourself and others about mental health issues: Learn about the common misconceptions and myths surrounding mental illness, and share accurate information with others to combat stigma.
- Seek support from trusted friends or family members: Talking to someone you trust can help reduce feelings of isolation and shame.
- Consider joining a support group: Support groups can provide a sense of community and understanding for those struggling with mental health issues.

- Seek professional help: A therapist or mental health professional can offer guidance and support in managing mental health issues and coping with feelings of shame or stigma.
- Practice self-care: Engage in activities that promote your mental health and well-being, such as exercise, meditation, or spending time in nature.

Importance of Seeking Help for Mental Health Concerns:
Seeking help for mental health concerns is critical in managing mental illness and improving overall well-being. Therapy, medication, and support groups can all be effective forms of treatment for mental health issues. By seeking help and support, we can reduce the impact of stigma and shame and improve our mental health and quality of life.

Personal Identity: Exploring the Complexity of Who We Are

Our identity is a complex and multifaceted concept encompassing our sense of self, values, beliefs, and experiences. Many factors, including upbringing, cultural background, gender identity, and life experiences, can influence personal identity.

This chapter will explore the different aspects of personal identity and how they shape who we are. We'll also discuss the importance of embracing our unique identity and the impact that this can have on our mental health and well-being.

Aspects of Personal Identity:

Personal identity can be broken down into several different aspects, including:

- Gender identity: Our sense of being male, female, or non-binary.
- Sexual orientation: Our romantic and sexual attraction to others.
- Cultural identity: Our connection to a particular culture or ethnic group.
- Religious identity: Our beliefs and practices related to religion or spirituality.
- Personality traits: Our unique patterns of thinking, feeling,

and behaving.

- Life experiences: Our past experiences, both positive and negative, and how they shape our sense of self.

Embracing Personal Identity:

Embracing our identity is essential in improving our mental health and well-being. When we deny or suppress aspects of our identity, we may experience feelings of shame, guilt, or disconnection. However, embracing individuality can help us feel more connected to ourselves and others and promote self-acceptance and self-esteem.

Remembering that personal identity is fluid and can change over time is essential. Exploring and embracing our identity is a lifelong process that can be challenging and rewarding.

Strategies for Embracing Personal Identity:

If you're struggling to embrace your identity, here are some strategies that may be helpful:

- Practice self-reflection: Reflect on your values, beliefs, and experiences and how they shape your sense of self.
- Seek support: Talk to friends, family, or a therapist who can offer support and understanding as you explore your identity.
- Connect with others who share your identity: Join a support group or community organization focusing on your identity.
- Engage in activities that promote self-expression: Explore hobbies or creative activities that allow you to express your unique identity.
- Challenge internalized biases: Work to challenge internalized biases and negative beliefs that may be holding you back from embracing your identity.

By embracing our identity, we can improve our mental health and well-being and feel more connected to ourselves and others.

Relationships: Navigating the Complexities of Human Connection

Human relationships can be both rewarding and challenging. Our relationships with others can impact our mental health and well-being and shape our sense of self and personal identity. In this chapter, we'll explore the different types of relationships we have with others and offer strategies for navigating the complexities of human connection.

Types of Relationships:

We have many different kinds of relationships in our lives, including:

- Family relationships: Our connections with family members, including parents, siblings, and extended family.
- Romantic relationships: Our intimate connections with romantic partners.
- Friendships: Our connections with close friends.
- Professional relationships: Our connections with colleagues and coworkers.
- Community relationships: Our connections with people in our communities, such as neighbors or fellow members of a faith community.

Challenges in Relationships:

While relationships can be rewarding, they can also be challenging. Some common challenges in relationships include:

- Communication issues: Misunderstandings, conflicts, and breakdowns in communication can all impact the quality of our relationships.
- Power imbalances: Relationships can become strained when one person holds more power or control than another.
- Trust issues: Trust is critical to any healthy relationship but can be challenging to establish and maintain.
- Conflict resolution: Disagreements are normal in any relationship, but resolving conflicts healthily and productively can be difficult.

Strategies for Navigating Relationships:

Navigating relationships can be challenging, but there are steps you can take to improve the quality of your connections with others:

- Practice active listening: Listen to what others say without judgment or interruption, and try to understand their perspective.
- Set healthy boundaries: Establish boundaries with others to protect your well-being and prevent conflicts.
- Build trust: Be consistent, honest, and reliable in your interactions with others to build trust and strengthen relationships.
- Practice conflict resolution: Use constructive communication techniques to resolve conflicts healthily and productively.

- Seek professional help: If you're struggling with relationship issues, consider seeking help from a therapist or counselor who can offer guidance and support.

By navigating the complexities of human relationships, we can improve the quality of our connections with others and promote our mental health and well-being.

Self-Compassion: The Importance of Kindness and Understanding Towards Ourselves

Self-compassion involves treating ourselves with kindness and understanding, just as we treat a close friend or loved one. While self-compassion may not come naturally to everyone, it can be valuable in promoting our mental health and well-being.

In this chapter, we'll explore the importance of self-compassion, the benefits it can offer, and offer strategies for cultivating self-compassion in our lives.

Importance of Self-Compassion:

Self-compassion involves treating ourselves with kindness and understanding, even when we make mistakes or experience challenges. It can help us feel more self-accepting, boost our self-esteem, and reduce stress and anxiety.

Unfortunately, many people struggle with self-criticism and negative self-talk, undermining their mental health and well-being. By practicing self-compassion, we can learn to be more gentle and forgiving towards ourselves and improve our overall quality of life.

Benefits of Self-Compassion:

Some of the benefits of practicing self-compassion include

the following:

- Increased self-esteem and self-worth
- Reduced stress and anxiety
- Greater emotional resilience
- Improved relationships with others
- Enhanced ability to cope with challenges and setbacks

Strategies for Cultivating Self-Compassion:

If you're struggling with self-compassion, here are some strategies that may be helpful:

- Practice mindfulness: Be present with your thoughts and feelings, and observe them without judgment or criticism.
- Treat yourself with kindness: Be gentle and understanding towards yourself, just as you would be with a close friend or loved one.
- Challenge negative self-talk: Identify negative thoughts and beliefs, and challenge them with evidence or a more positive perspective.
- Cultivate gratitude: Focus on the positive aspects of your life, and practice gratitude for the good things you have.
- Seek support: Talk to a therapist or counselor who can help you develop self-compassion and coping strategies.

By cultivating self-compassion, we can improve our mental health and well-being and live more fulfilling lives.

Stress Management: Strategies for Coping with Life's Challenges

Stress is a normal part of life, but it can negatively affect our mental and physical health when it becomes overwhelming or chronic. In this chapter, we'll explore the impact of stress on our well-being and offer strategies for managing stress and coping with life's challenges.

Impact of Stress on Our Well-being:

Stress can impact our mental and physical health in a variety of ways. It can lead to feelings of anxiety, depression, and burnout and can also cause physical symptoms such as headaches, fatigue, and digestive issues. Prolonged stress can weaken the immune system, making us more vulnerable to illness and disease.

Stress can also impact our relationships and work performance. When stressed, we may be less patient, less attentive, and less effective in our daily tasks. This can lead to conflict and tension in our relationships and may impact our job performance.

Strategies for Managing Stress:

If you're struggling with stress, there are steps you can take to manage it and cope with life's challenges:

- Practice relaxation techniques: Engage in activities that promote relaxation and stress reduction, such as meditation, yoga, or deep breathing exercises.
- Exercise regularly: Regular exercise can help reduce stress and improve overall well-being.
- Practice good sleep hygiene: Prioritize getting enough restful sleep each night to support your physical and mental health.
- Connect with others: Talk to friends, family, or a therapist who can offer support and understanding as you cope with stress.
- Practice time management: Prioritize your tasks and schedule your time effectively to reduce stress and increase productivity.
- Set healthy boundaries: Establish boundaries with others to protect your well-being and prevent conflicts.
- Seek professional help: If you're struggling with chronic or overwhelming stress, consider seeking help from a therapist or counselor who can offer guidance and support.

By managing stress and coping with life's challenges, we can improve our mental and physical health and live more fulfilling lives.

In addition to the strategies listed above, here are some additional tips for managing stress:

- Focus on what you can control: While we can't always control external factors that cause stress, we can control our response.
- Practice gratitude: Focus on the positive aspects of your life, and practice gratitude for the good things you have.

- Use humor: Laughing and finding humor in situations can help reduce stress and improve mood.
- Practice self-care: Take time to engage in activities that bring you joy and promote your well-being, such as spending time in nature or pursuing a hobby.
- Consider therapy: Therapy can help you learn coping strategies and develop resilience in the face of stress.

By incorporating these strategies into your daily life, you can better manage stress and improve your overall well-being.

Grief and Loss: Navigating the Emotional Landscape of Loss

Grief and loss are universal experiences that can be incredibly challenging to navigate. Whether we're mourning the loss of a loved one, a job, or a relationship, the emotional impact of loss can be significant.

In this chapter, we'll explore the emotional landscape of grief and loss and offer strategies for coping with these difficult experiences.

Emotional Landscape of Grief and Loss:

Grief and loss can bring up a range of emotions, including:

- Sadness: Feeling a deep sense of sadness and sorrow over the loss.
- Anger: Feeling angry or resentful about the loss or anger towards others or oneself.
- Guilt: Feeling guilty about the loss or feeling like something more could have been done to prevent it.
- Anxiety: Feeling anxious about the future or worrying about what comes next.
- Numbness: Feeling emotionally numb or disconnected from others.

These emotions can be overwhelming and challenging to process, but it's important to remember that they are a normal and natural part of the grieving process.

Strategies for Coping with Grief and Loss:

If you're struggling with grief and loss, here are some strategies that may be helpful:

- Allow yourself to feel your emotions: Expressing rather than suppressing or denying them.
- Seek support: Talk to friends, family, or a therapist who can offer support and understanding as you navigate the grieving process.
- Practice self-care: Engage in activities that promote physical and emotional well-being, such as exercise, meditation, or spending time in nature.
- Find healthy ways to cope: Consider healthy coping strategies, such as journaling, creative expression, or volunteering.
- Join a support group: Consider joining a support group for grieving people. Support groups can provide community and understanding for those struggling with loss.
- Seek professional help: If you're struggling with the emotional impact of loss, consider seeking help from a therapist or counselor who can offer guidance and support.

By acknowledging and processing our emotions, seeking support, and finding healthy ways to cope, we can navigate the emotional landscape of grief and loss and move forward with a renewed sense of strength and resilience.

Emotional Intelligence: Understanding and Managing Our Emotions

Emotional intelligence involves the ability to understand and manage our own emotions and recognize and respond to the feelings of others. It's a valuable skill that can help us navigate relationships, work effectively with others, and promote our mental health and well-being.

In this chapter, we'll explore the concept of emotional intelligence and its importance and offer strategies for developing and improving it.

Understanding Emotional Intelligence:

Emotional intelligence involves several different skills, including:

- Self-awareness: The ability to recognize and understand our emotions and how they impact our thoughts and behaviors.
- Self-regulation: The ability to manage emotions and impulses and respond appropriately to situations.
- Motivation: The ability to set goals and motivate ourselves towards achieving them.
- Empathy: The ability to recognize and understand the emotions of others and respond appropriately.

- Social skills: The ability to communicate effectively with others, build relationships, and work collaboratively.

Importance of Emotional Intelligence:
Emotional intelligence is an essential skill that can have numerous benefits for our personal and professional lives, including:

- Improved relationships with others
- Greater emotional resilience
- Enhanced ability to cope with stress and challenges
- Improved communication and conflict-resolution skills
- Increased self-awareness and self-understanding

Strategies for Developing Emotional Intelligence:
If you're looking to improve your emotional intelligence, here are some strategies that may be helpful:

- Practice self-reflection: Reflect on your emotions, reactions, and behaviors and how they impact your relationships and interactions with others.
- Practice mindfulness: Engage in mindfulness practices, such as meditation or deep breathing exercises, to develop self-awareness and regulate emotions.
- Seek feedback: Ask for feedback from others on improving your communication and interpersonal skills.
- Practice empathy: Try to put yourself in the shoes of others and understand their emotions and perspectives.
- Build positive relationships: Invest time and effort in building positive relationships with others, and improve your communication and conflict resolution skills.

- Seek professional help: Consider working with a therapist or counselor who can help you develop and improve your emotional intelligence.

Developing and improving our emotional intelligence can enhance our relationships, promote our mental health and well-being, and improve our overall quality of life.

Mindfulness: Cultivating Awareness and Presence in Our Lives

Mindfulness involves cultivating awareness and presence in our lives and being fully present in the present moment. It's a valuable skill that can help us reduce stress, increase focus and concentration, and improve our overall well-being.

In this chapter, we'll explore the concept of mindfulness and its benefits and offer strategies for cultivating mindfulness in our lives.

Understanding Mindfulness:

Mindfulness involves being fully present in the present moment without judgment or distraction. It consists of bringing our attention to our thoughts, feelings, and sensations and observing them without getting caught up. It's a way of being that can help us develop greater awareness and understanding of ourselves and our surroundings.

Benefits of Mindfulness:

Some of the benefits of practicing mindfulness include the following:

- Reduced stress and anxiety
- Improved focus and concentration
- Increased emotional regulation and resilience

- Improved sleep quality
- Enhanced relationships and communication skills

Strategies for Cultivating Mindfulness:

If you're interested in practicing mindfulness, here are some strategies that may be helpful:

- Practice mindfulness meditation: Engage in daily mindfulness meditation practice, focusing your attention on your breath or a specific object, and observing your thoughts and feelings without judgment.
- Practice mindful breathing: Take time throughout the day to focus on breathing and bring your attention back to your breath when your mind wanders.
- Engage in mindful activities: Engage in activities that promote mindfulness and presence, such as yoga, tai chi, or mindful walking.
- Practice gratitude: Take time each day to reflect on the positive aspects of your life and express gratitude for them.
- Use technology mindfully: Practice mindfully using technology, taking breaks from screens, and focusing on the present moment.
- Seek professional help: Consider working with a therapist or counselor who can help you develop and maintain a mindfulness practice.

By cultivating mindfulness, we can reduce stress, increase focus and concentration, and improve our overall well-being.

Cognitive Behavioral Therapy: Changing Our Thoughts and Behaviors for Improved Mental Health

Cognitive Behavioral Therapy (CBT) is a type of therapy that focuses on changing our thoughts and behaviors to improve our mental health and well-being. It's a highly effective therapy that can help individuals overcome various mental health challenges, including anxiety, depression, and trauma.

In this chapter, we'll explore the concept of CBT and its benefits and offer strategies for incorporating CBT into our lives.

Understanding Cognitive Behavioral Therapy:

CBT is based on the idea that our thoughts, feelings, and behaviors are interconnected and that we can impact others by changing one. It involves identifying negative thought patterns and beliefs that may contribute to our mental health challenges and replacing them with more positive and helpful ones.

Benefits of Cognitive Behavioral Therapy:

Some of the benefits of CBT include the following:

- Reduced symptoms of anxiety, depression, and other mental health challenges
- Improved coping skills and resilience

- Enhanced problem-solving and decision-making abilities
- Improved relationships and communication skills
- Increased self-awareness and self-understanding

Strategies for Incorporating CBT:

If you're interested in incorporating CBT into your life, here are some strategies that may be helpful:

- Identify negative thought patterns: Pay attention to negative thoughts or beliefs contributing to your mental health challenges, and challenge them with more positive and helpful ones.
- Practice behavioral activation: Engage in activities that bring you pleasure and satisfaction, even when you don't feel like it.
- Develop coping skills: Identify healthy coping strategies, such as deep breathing or progressive muscle relaxation, and practice them when feeling stressed or overwhelmed.
- Seek professional help: Consider working with a therapist or counselor specializing in CBT, who can help you identify and change negative thought patterns and behaviors.

By incorporating CBT into our lives, we can improve our mental health and well-being and develop greater resilience and coping skills in the face of challenges.

Resilience: Building Inner Strength in the Face of Adversity

Resilience involves the ability to bounce back from adversity and adapt to new situations and challenges. It's a valuable skill that can help us overcome difficult circumstances and improve our mental and emotional well-being.

In this chapter, we'll explore the concept of resilience and its benefits and offer strategies for building resilience.

Understanding Resilience:

Resilience involves building strength and resources to help us cope with difficult situations and challenges. It involves developing a positive mindset, strong social connections, and healthy coping strategies.

Benefits of Resilience:

Some of the benefits of building resilience include the following:

- Improved mental and emotional well-being
- Greater adaptability to new situations and challenges
- Increased self-confidence and self-esteem
- Enhanced problem-solving and decision-making abilities
- Stronger social connections and support network

Strategies for Building Resilience:

If you're interested in building resilience in your life, here are some strategies that may be helpful:

- Cultivate a positive mindset: Practice positive self-talk and focus on your strengths and accomplishments rather than dwelling on mistakes or failures.
- Build solid social connections: Invest time and effort in building positive relationships with others, and seek support and guidance from friends and family when facing challenges.
- Practice self-care: Take time to engage in activities that promote your physical and emotional well-being, such as exercise, mindfulness, or spending time in nature.
- Develop healthy coping skills: Identify healthy coping strategies, such as journaling or deep breathing exercises, and practice them regularly to manage stress and anxiety.
- Find purpose and meaning: Identify your values and goals, and find ways to align your daily life with them.
- Seek professional help: If you're struggling with mental health challenges or facing significant adversity, consider seeking help from a therapist or counselor who can offer guidance and support.

Building resilience can develop strength and adaptability and improve mental and emotional well-being.

Self-Compassion: Learning to Treat Ourselves with Kindness and Understanding

Self-compassion involves treating ourselves with kindness and understanding rather than self-criticism or judgment. It's a valuable skill that can help us improve our self-esteem, reduce stress and anxiety, and promote our overall well-being.

In this chapter, we'll explore the concept of self-compassion and its benefits and offer strategies for cultivating self-compassion in our lives.

Understanding Self-Compassion:

Self-compassion involves treating ourselves with the same kindness, concern, and understanding we would offer to a good friend. It consists in recognizing our imperfections and mistakes and responding with compassion and understanding rather than harsh self-criticism.

Benefits of Self-Compassion:

Some of the benefits of cultivating self-compassion include:

- Improved self-esteem and self-worth
- Reduced stress and anxiety
- Enhanced resilience and coping skills

- Improved relationships with others
- Increased self-awareness and self-understanding

Strategies for Cultivating Self-Compassion:

If you're interested in cultivating self-compassion in your life, here are some strategies that may be helpful:

- Practice mindfulness: Engage in mindfulness practices, such as meditation or deep breathing exercises, to develop self-awareness and regulate emotions.
- Practice self-kindness: Treat yourself with kindness and understanding rather than harsh self-criticism or judgment.
- Practice self-acceptance: Recognize and accept your imperfections and mistakes, and respond with compassion and understanding.
- Seek support: Seek support and guidance from friends, family, or a therapist who can offer understanding and support.
- Develop healthy coping skills: Identify healthy coping strategies, such as exercise, creative expression, or spending time in nature, and practice them regularly.
- Practice gratitude: Take time each day to reflect on the positive aspects of your life and express gratitude for them.

By cultivating self-compassion, we can improve our mental and emotional well-being, reduce stress and anxiety, and develop greater resilience and coping skills in the face of challenges.

Conclusion

In "The Secret Lives of Ordinary People," we've explored various personal growth and well-being topics. Each chapter offers valuable insights and strategies for cultivating inner strength and well-being, from understanding and managing our emotions to building resilience and self-compassion.

Through this exploration, we've learned that personal growth and well-being are ongoing processes that require patience, perseverance, and self-compassion. By developing a greater understanding of ourselves and our experiences and practicing healthy coping strategies and self-care, we can overcome challenges and promote our overall well-being.

It's important to remember that seeking help and support is a sign of strength, not weakness. Whether working with a therapist or counselor or seeking guidance and support from friends and family, many resources are available to help us on our personal growth journeys.

Ultimately, we can create a more fulfilling and meaningful life by embracing our unique experiences and cultivating compassion and understanding for ourselves and others. Thank you for joining us on this journey of personal growth and self-discovery.

Afterword

Thank you for taking the time to read "The Secret Lives of Ordinary People." I hope the book offers valuable insights and practical guidance for cultivating inner strength and resilience.

As you've read through the different chapters, you may have noticed that personal growth and well-being are ongoing processes. There are no quick fixes or easy solutions but a commitment to constant self-reflection, learning, and growth.

Remember that everyone has their unique journey, and there is no one-size-fits-all approach to personal growth. What works for one person may not work for another. However, the strategies and insights presented in this book offer a starting point to explore what works best for you.

I encourage you to continue your growth journey, seek help and support when needed, and cultivate self-compassion to improve your well-being and create a more compassionate and understanding world.

Thank you again for joining me on this journey of personal growth and self-discovery.